3/09

Fact Finders®

EXTREME LIFE

FLESH-EATING MACHINES

MAGGOTS IN THE FOOD CHAIN

BY JUNE PRESZLER

Consultant:
Gary A. Dunn, M.S.
Director of Education
Young Entomologists' Society Inc.
Minibeast Zooseum and Education Center
Lansing, Michigan

Capstone
press®

Mankato, Minnesota

Fact Finders are published by Capstone Press,
151 Good Counsel Drive, P.O. Box 669, Mankato, Minnesota 56002.
www.capstonepress.com

Library of Congress Cataloging-in-Publication Data
Preszler, June, 1954–
    Flesh-eating machines: maggots in the food chain/by June Preszler.
    p. cm. — (Fact finders. Extreme life)
    Summary: "Describes the world of maggots, including characteristics, life cycle, and their role
in the food chain" — Provided by publisher.
    Includes bibliographical references and index.
    ISBN-13: 978-1-4296-1263-0 (hardcover)
    ISBN-10: 1-4296-1263-0 (hardcover)
    1. Maggots — Juvenile literature. 2. Food chains (Ecology) — Juvenile literature. I. Title.
II. Series.
QL533.2.P74 2008
595.77'139 — dc22   2007033252

Editorial Credits

Megan Schoeneberger and Christine Peterson, editors;
    Alison Thiele, designer; Linda Clavel, photo researcher

Photo Credits

Ardea/Andy Teare, cover; Ardea/Jean Michel Labat, 13; Capstone Press/Karon Dubke, 20, 28;
Corbis/Joe McDonald, 11; iStockphoto/Benjamin Schepp, 15 (top); Nature Picture Library/Kim
Taylor, 12, 18; Peter Arnold/Darlyne A. Murawski, 5; Photo Researchers Inc./Eye of Science, 17;
Photo Researchers Inc./Pascal Goetgheluck, 29; Photo Researchers Inc./Scott Camazine, 23; Photo
Researchers Inc./Volker Steger, 26; Shutterstock/Andy Heyward, 9 (notebook); Shutterstock/Feng
Yu, 14; Shutterstock/fotosav, 7 (grass); Shutterstock/Helder Joaquim Soares de Almeida, 7 (paper);
Shutterstock/William Attard McCarthy, 7 (deer); University of California, Davis/Kathy Keatley
Garvey, 15 (bottom); Visuals Unlimited/Bill Beatty, 21; Visuals Unlimited/Dr. James L. Castner, 7
(deer remains), 7 (bottle fly), 8, 19, 25, 27; Visuals Unlimited/Nigel Cattlin, 9 (bottom); Wikipedia,
public-domain image, 9 (top)

1 2 3 4 5 6 13 12 11 10 09 08

TABLE OF CONTENTS

CHAPTER 1

MAGGOT DELIGHT

The worms crawl in; the worms crawl out.
In your ears and out your snout.
They eat your eyes. They eat your nose.
They eat the jelly between your toes.

— *popular children's rhyme*

Can't you just picture those slimy, squishy peg-shaped worms crawling in and out of a dead body? But those tiny creatures crawling in, on, and around dead bodies aren't really worms at all. You've just had your first introduction to the disgusting, wriggling, and thoroughly amazing world of maggots.

GROSS!

Scientists once counted more than 48,500 maggots on about ⅓ pound (151 grams) of meat.

Maggots wriggle and squirm as they eat their way through flesh.

Maggots and the Food Chain

    Maggots just love to lunch on flesh. These **decomposers** are one link in nature's amazing food chain. All living things get energy and nutrients from the food chain.

    Here's how it works. Wild berries and other plants grow on bushes near the edge of a forest. Plants are producers at the bottom of the food chain. They change sunlight into chemical energy that helps them grow.

    Next, a hungry deer spies berries sparkling in the sun and begins to eat. Animals like the deer are called consumers. They get energy and nutrients from plants and other producers.

decomposers: Organisms like maggots that break down dead things into nutrients plants need to grow

PRODUCER

Turns sunlight into energy.

DECOMPOSER

Gets energy from the dead flesh
and returns nutrients to the soil.

CONSUMER

Gets energy by eating
the producer.

CONSUMER DIES

Flies lay eggs on dead animals. Maggots hatch from the eggs and begin eating the flesh.

As the deer eats, it is frightened by a sound in the woods. The deer leaps across a nearby road. The frightened deer doesn't notice an oncoming car. The car strikes and kills the deer.

In death, the deer becomes food for scavengers and decomposers. Within minutes, flies land on the deer carcass. The flies lay eggs that turn into maggots. Maggots get energy by clearing away or eating the dead meat. Maggots and other decomposers break down flesh, which returns nutrients to the soil.

SAY CHEESE!

Ever heard of someone eating maggots on purpose? Well, it happens quite frequently on the small island of Sardinia near Italy. Many folks enjoy a tasty treat of maggot cheese. Stuffed with maggots, the cheese seems to wriggle and ooze. But cheese-eaters beware. Maggots spring from the cheese and could get in your eyes. By the way, eating this disgusting cheese is also against the law. Island officials say cheese crawling with maggots can't possibly meet health standards.

As they eat, maggots turn dead flesh into nutrients for plants.

CHAPTER 2

FROM MAGGOT TO HOUSE FLY

Look at that house fly buzzing around your face. That fly hasn't always had wings. It used to be a wingless, wriggling maggot. Maggots are the **larvae** that develop after ordinary flies like bottle flies or blow flies lay their eggs. That's right. Maggots come from and become flies.

Once a fly has found a landing spot, it quickly begins to work. A single blow fly can lay up to 300 eggs at one time. In anywhere from eight to 20 hours, the eggs will hatch into larvae or maggots.

larva: a worm-like insect that has hatched from its egg

Flies can't resist dead animals. They lay eggs in the dead flesh. The eggs hatch and become munching maggots.

GROSS!

Fly larvae look like slithering, squishy lumps, but they are really hungry maggots ready to eat and eat and eat.

When they hatch, maggots are white, skinny, and very tiny. Within 24 hours, maggots molt or shed an outer covering called a cuticle. For the next five days, maggots eat and grow to about ½ to ¾ of an inch long (1.27 to 1.91 centimeters). A full-grown maggot is about the size of a Tic-Tac.

At pupa stage, maggots look dark and crusty.

No Butterflies Here

A maggot's skin color darkens as it grows. After about 10 days, the brown-colored maggots leave their feeding area and search for a drier spot where they'll pupate.

When a maggot pupates, a capsule forms. The maggot itself rests inside the capsule and no longer moves. But inside the capsule the maggot's body changes. Maggots don't turn into anything as pretty as butterflies. Nope, they become ordinary flies.

Top 5 Amazing Maggot Facts!

(1) Not all maggots are white and tiny. Scientists believe there are at least 90,000 different types of maggots and each one is a little bit different.

(2) Many people who fish prefer maggots to earthworms as bait. In fact, in the United Kingdom maggots are so popular with anglers that they can be purchased 24 hours a day from special vending machines named Mag-It!

(3) Maggots as artists? You bet! In 2007, a Sacramento, California, art exhibit featured artwork created by squiggling, swooping lines of maggots.

(4) Got some maggots you want to get rid of? Well, there are a couple of tricks. Maggots slide away from spices like salt, cloves, and even bay leaves.

(5) While most maggots eat dead animals, some prefer living things like humans. Bot flies lay their eggs on animals. The eggs hatch and latch onto mosquitoes drinking blood. The mosquitoes carry a few tiny maggots to humans. The maggots drop off, burrow into human flesh, and begin to eat. After six weeks, the plump maggots eat their way out of the skin, fall to the ground, and pupate.

GROSS!

Flies can lay eggs in an animal! A fly swoops into an animal's mouth and down its throat. Soon, maggots grow in its belly. Yuck!

CHAPTER 3

DINNER TIME!

Maggots are amazing flesh-eating machines. They tunnel through food by wriggling or flipping their bodies. While they eat, they store the energy they need to grow and change into flies.

Maggot bodies are soft, squishy, and mostly peg-shaped. Their bodies narrow toward the front. The front end has little hooks that work like rakes to pull in decaying flesh. Since maggots don't have jaws or teeth, they can't chew their food. Instead, they make a juice that dissolves the food so they can digest it.

GROSS!

When maggots get really hungry, they'll even eat each other!

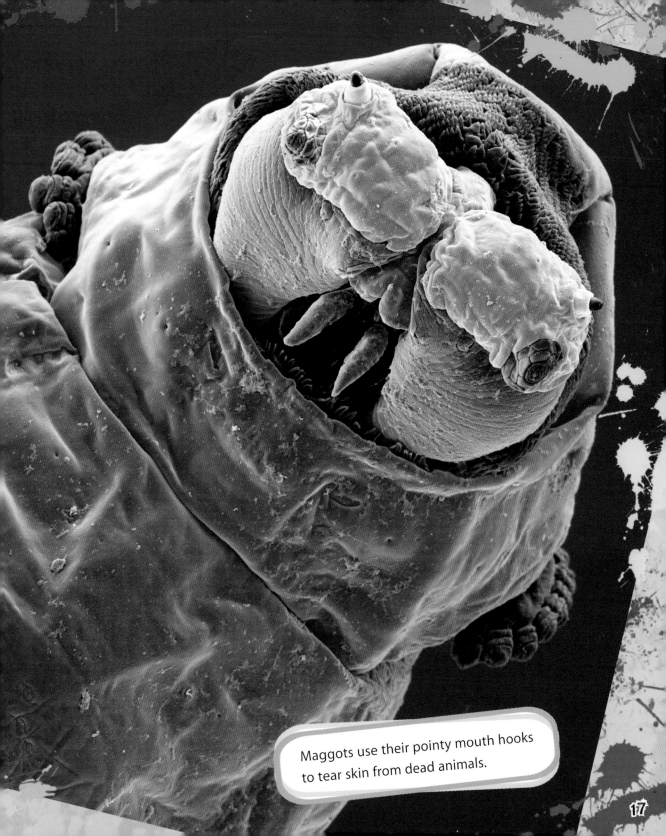

Maggots use their pointy mouth hooks to tear skin from dead animals.

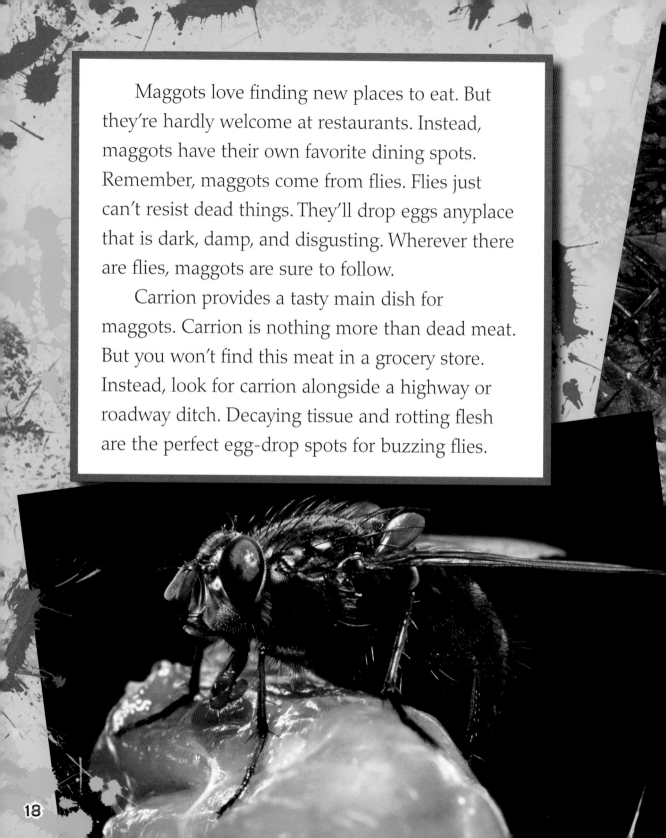

Maggots love finding new places to eat. But they're hardly welcome at restaurants. Instead, maggots have their own favorite dining spots. Remember, maggots come from flies. Flies just can't resist dead things. They'll drop eggs anyplace that is dark, damp, and disgusting. Wherever there are flies, maggots are sure to follow.

Carrion provides a tasty main dish for maggots. Carrion is nothing more than dead meat. But you won't find this meat in a grocery store. Instead, look for carrion alongside a highway or roadway ditch. Decaying tissue and rotting flesh are the perfect egg-drop spots for buzzing flies.

ROADKILL STEW

If you're a maggot, you'll love this roadkill stew!

SERVES: Thousands of maggots

INGREDIENTS: One decaying carcass
A deer, squirrel, or bird will do just fine.

STEPS:

1. After hatching on the dead carcass, begin tearing at the flesh with your hooks.
2. Release a disgusting juice-like liquid making sure the decaying meat is completely covered.
3. Wriggle around until the meat becomes a soupy mess.
4. Gather thousands of your maggot friends and enjoy!

The Sweet Taste of Garbage

On the menu today is a lovely buffet of rotten eggs, moldy cheese, and an extra helping of month-old tuna salad. Sound delicious? It does if you're a maggot. Flies love to lay eggs in a pile of stinky, rotting garbage. When they hatch, maggots enjoy their first meal of smelly, yet tasty, garbage.

dung: Dung is just a science word for good old-fashioned poop.

Tasty Poop

Animal **dung** is another favorite dining spot for maggots. That's right. Maggots also eat poop. It's warm, smelly, and full of nutrients. What's not to love? Check your backyard. If you don't clean up after your dog, you're sure to find maggots crawling all about the poop.

INTERVIEW WITH A BLOW FLY MAGGOT

INTERVIEWER: Whew! It's hot around here. What's causing the heat wave?

MAGGOT: It's just us maggots at work. It's not easy breaking down a rotting carcass.

INTERVIEWER: But why is it so hot on the job?

MAGGOT: It's all that wriggling and tunneling we do. The heat helps us quickly break down the flesh. In fact, we can reduce a 50-pound (22.7-kilogram) carcass to skin and bones in four to five days during hot summer weather.

INTERVIEWER: Don't you guys ever take a break?

MAGGOT: Sometimes we move to the outer edges in order to cool down, but we never stop working. In fact, it's back to work for me. Gotta fly!

Watch Out!

A maggot's eating habits are sometimes the cause of its own death. As maggots work their way through a carcass, they often become snack material. Larger scavengers feast on carrion too.

Screwworm maggots plunge into skin with their mouthparts down, often creating a large wound. People and animals have died from these sores.

Bears, raccoons, vultures, and seagulls love to munch on wriggling maggots they find on bits of carcass. Rove beetles, carrion beetles, soldier flies, and other insects also love to feast on maggots.

CHAPTER 4

MAGGOTS AT WORK

Maggots aren't only on the job in the world of nature. Maggots also play a helping hand at crime scenes and in hospitals.

These tiny creatures are often found at a crime scene, especially if there's a dead body involved. Maggots are mini crime scene investigators. Maggots tunneling through a **corpse** can reveal information about the crime. Investigators sometimes find maggots on a dead body. Investigators then know that the person has been dead for about eight to 20 hours. That's how long it takes maggots to hatch after flies have laid their eggs.

You won't find maggots resting on the job. Busy maggots can increase the temperature of a corpse by up to 127.4 degrees Fahrenheit (53 degrees Celsius).

corpse: a dead body — usually a person's body rather than an animal's.

GROSS!

When a gang of maggots takes over a corpse, they sometimes make it seem like the dead body is breathing and moving.

25

When regular medicine fails, some doctors turn to maggots. Maggots work as healing agents. They gobble up the bacteria that cause infections. Maggots sometimes get so full of dead tissue that they grow to three to four times their original size.

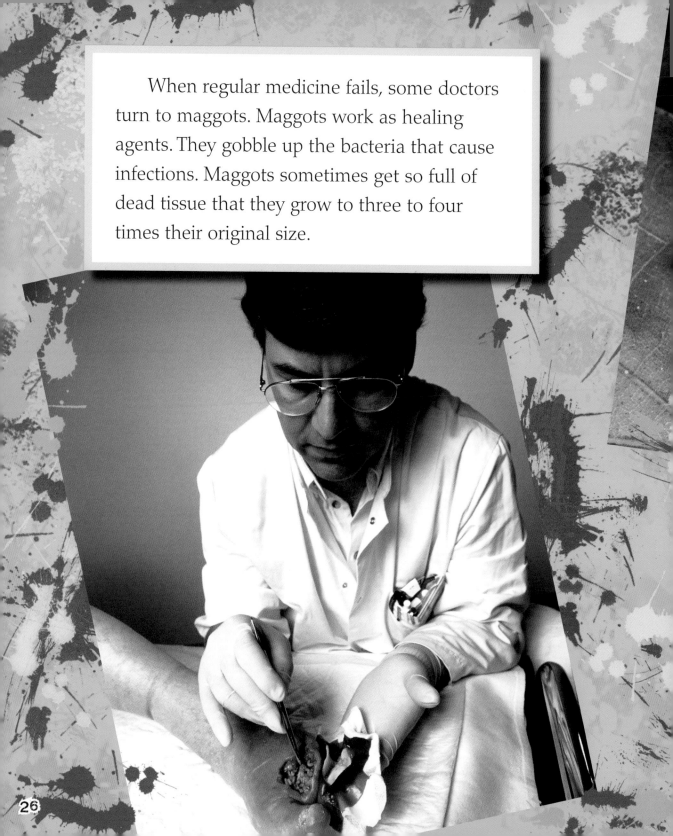

debris: Remaining or leftover waste. Debris is garbage, rotting animal carcass, or poop.

Amazing Maggots

Maggots may look gross as they wriggle through flesh, but they're really doing us a favor. Maggots and other decomposers work around the clock clearing away dead and rotting **debris**. Without maggots and other decomposers, the world would be overrun with rotting, smelling, disgusting stuff. Not a pretty picture. So don't think of maggots as disgusting flesh-eaters. Think of them as one small part of nature's amazing clean-up crew.

TRUE LIVES OF SCIENTISTS

Specially trained bug scientists called forensic **entomologists** sometimes help police detectives and crime scene investigators solve crimes. They don't just study bugs and maggots on dead bodies. They study the bugs pasted to windshields on cars involved in hit-and-run accidents. They pick maggots from ketchup in food poisoning cases. And, of course, they study maggots inside corpses.

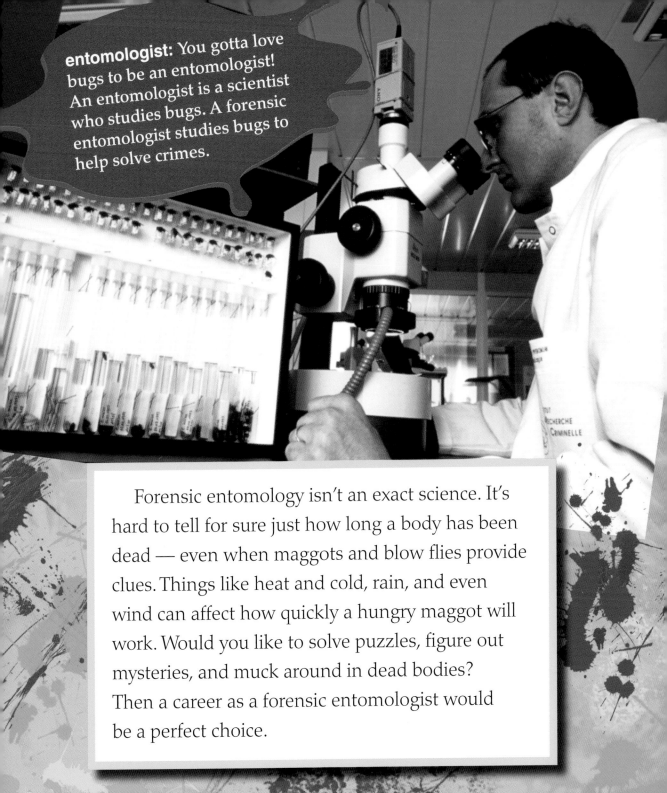

Forensic entomology isn't an exact science. It's hard to tell for sure just how long a body has been dead — even when maggots and blow flies provide clues. Things like heat and cold, rain, and even wind can affect how quickly a hungry maggot will work. Would you like to solve puzzles, figure out mysteries, and muck around in dead bodies? Then a career as a forensic entomologist would be a perfect choice.

GLOSSARY

BLOW FLY (BLOH FLYE) — large usually hairy metallic blue or green fly that lays eggs in carrion or dung or wounds

CARRION (KARE-ee-uhn) — dead animal flesh

CONSUMER (kuhn-SOO-mur) — an animal that eats plants or other animals for energy

CORPSE (KORPS) — a dead body

DEBRIS (duh-BREE) — leftover animal waste or garbage

DECOMPOSER (dee-kuhm-PO-zur) — a living thing that turns dead things into food for others

DUNG (DUHNG) — solid waste from animals

ENTOMOLOGIST (en-tuh-MAH-luh-jist) — a scientist who studies insects

LARVA (LAR-vuh) — an insect at the stage of development between an egg and a pupa; more than one larva are larvae.

PUPATE (PYOO-peyt) — the process in which an insect changes from a larva into an adult

INTERNET SITES

FactHound offers a safe, fun way to find Internet sites related to this book. All of the sites on FactHound have been researched by our staff.

Here's how:

1. Visit *www.facthound.com*

2. Choose your grade level.

3. Type in this book ID **1429612630** for age-appropriate sites. You may also browse subjects by clicking on letters, or by clicking on pictures and words.

4. Click on the **Fetch It** button.

FactHound will fetch the best sites for you!

READ MORE

Denega, Danielle. *Gut-eating Bugs: Maggots Reveal the Time of Death!* 24/7: Science Behind the Scenes. New York: Franklin Watts, 2007.

Levete, Sarah. *Rot and Decay: A Story of Death, Scavengers, and Recycling*. Let's Explore Science. Vero Beach, Fla.: Rourke, 2008.

Wallace, Holly. *Food Chains and Webs*. Life Processes. Chicago: Heinemann, 2006.

INDEX